Moon Magic

Modern Guides to Ancient Wisdom

HERRON

Contents

Introduction

The moon is a constant, reliable presence in all our lives. While many of us no longer appreciate or sometimes even notice the celestial object in the night sky, its awe-inspiring, magical energy connects every single one of us.

It should come as no surprise that many cultures throughout time have had lunar deities. For millennia, humans have observed the changing face of the moon, honouring its power and wondering about its significance. The moon, which waxes and wanes in predictable cycles, was used to measure the passing of time, and has long been a symbol for birth, growth, death and renewal.

Although we have largely lost our deep and ancient connection to the moon, its power remains open to us all, if you know how to harness it. In this book you will learn some simple ways to work with the moon's divine, feminine energy through rituals, spellwork, meditations and mantras.

Firstly, use our 10 steps to moon magic to reconnect with the cosmos as well as connect more deeply with yourself. And whether you want to improve your health, your career or your relationships, every stage of the lunar cycle brings a new outlook and energy to your life that can be used to your benefit. This book will guide you through the four main moon phases to help bring your dreams and desires to life.

You'll be amazed at how much more you can achieve when you synchronise your activities with the moon.

Magical
Moon Facts

A 'supermoon' is when a full moon occurs at its closest point to Earth, making it appear larger and brighter

Some form of moon worship can be found in most ancient religions

The moon has its own time zone: Lunar Standard Time

Moonlight triggers a mass coral spawning in the Great Barrier Reef each year

The rise and fall of the tides on Earth is caused by the moon

The moon has long been associated with dreams, the subconscious realm and intuition

It's often said that more babies are born during the full moon, when the gravitational pull is the strongest

The word 'lunatic' comes from the connection between the moon and unusual behaviour

The moon is drifting 3.8cm away from us each year

Go slowly,
my lovely moon,
go slowly.

Khaled Hosseini

10 Steps to Moon Magic

—

*How you can live a better,
richer and more fulfilled life by tapping
into the energy of the moon*

Reconnect with Ancient Rhythms

If you've ever looked up at the night sky and felt a connection, then you'll intuitively understand the power inherent in the moon.

The moon, with its illuminating, perpetual cycle that ebbs and flows, is a powerful force that affects all of nature. It controls the tides and influences our emotions, regulates women's menstrual cycles and creates a rhythm that has guided humans for thousands of years.

Our ancestors were well aware of the moon's prominence and power, relying on it to inform and predict many aspects of life, from planting to hunting, navigating to fertility. Although most of us no longer have this connection to natural spirituality, you can still learn to harness the moon's immense power.

By taking just a second to look up into the night sky, you'll start to reconnect with the planet's ancient rhythms. As you gaze up, note what phase the moon is in and notice what's going on in your body, mind, heart and spirit. Unleash your primal instincts: howl at the moon, gaze at the stars, dance in the moonlight.

Think about how you feel at certain times of the lunar cycle and observe the ebb and flow of your energy. Are you calm? Dreamy? Contemplative? Ready for action? Make notes and read back on them each month to any notice patterns.

There's a lot to be learned when you succumb to the energy of the universe.

Keep Track of the Moon's Phases

Follow the cycles of the moon to set intentions, create more abundance and connect with your own inner wisdom.

The phases of the moon are caused by the position of the moon in relation to the sun. While the new moon is dictated by the proximity of the sun to the moon, the full moon occurs when they are at opposite positions in the sky. It takes just under one month – an average of 29.5 days – for the moon to complete all its phases.

It's important to gain an understanding of the lunar phases as each one affects our emotions and well-being in different ways and each one brings change and new perspectives. Although the lunar cycle has eight phases, in this book we'll be focussing on the powerful energies of the new moon, waxing moon, full moon and waning moon.

Once you're fully in tune with the moon's cycles, you'll understand when it is the right time to manifest your dreams, when you must find emotional balance and when you should rest and recharge.

How to track the lunar phases:

- Purchase a moon phase calendar or find a printable chart online.

- Download an app on your phone. There are many to choose from, but the most useful tell you the phases of the moon as well as the astrological sign the moon is travelling through on any day of the year.

- Journal and record what you see. In the southern hemisphere, a waxing moon looks like the letter C (it has a left curve) while the waning moon curves to the right.

THE MOON'S FOUR PRIMARY PHASES:

New Moon

Waxing Moon

Full Moon

Waning Moon

The moon is a reminder that no matter what phase I am in, I am still whole.

Weave Moon Magic into Your Life

Actively harness the moon's powerful energy and live in accordance with the rhythms of the universe.

- Check in with the lunar cycle, and observe any fluctuations in your mood. The moon reminds us that change is a constant.

- Plan a little ritual for each new moon.

- Dance under the moon like no one is watching.

- Set out your crystals to clear their energy.

- Draw tarot cards.

- Make a crystal grid.

- Take a hike under the light of the full moon.

- Simply stand outside under a full moon and bathe in the light.

- Write reflections in your journal.

- Meditate on the cycles of our planet and the vastness of the universe.

- Choose one phase of the moon to be your special time and get creative.

Create a Moon Garden

*Bring the moon to your backyard by creating
a silver-and-white homage to its ethereal beauty.*

Ancient wisdom once held that flowers and herbs were more powerful if gathered by the light of the moon. Whether or not that's true, some plants are indeed more fragrant or beautiful after dusk in order to attract night-time pollinators. And with many of us out of the house during the day, creating a moon garden that can be enjoyed during the evening or by the light of the moon can bring untold joy and pleasure to your life.

PICK YOUR SITE

Choose anything from a small garden bed to a larger plot but make sure that it is exposed to moonlight. If possible, ensure it's near your deck, balcony or a large window from where the sights, sounds and smells of the garden can be easily enjoyed.

WHAT TO PLANT

Plant white or lightly coloured blooms that open at night and silverleaf shrubs and ghostly white trees that will shimmer in the dappled moonlight. Shiny-leaved sculptural plants add form and shadow, while evening-fragrant flowers like jasmine and gardenias bring olfactory enchantment.

WHAT ELSE TO CONSIDER

A moonlight garden of silver and white should combine beauty and practicality. Add white rocks and reflective hangings to illuminate your path; a water feature will add soothing sounds.

Use the Moon Cycles to Realise Your Dreams

*Set aside some time to assess your goals in life,
and use the lunar cycles to manifest them.*

NEW MOON

The new moon is auspicious as the dark sky can be filled with the light of your intentions. Use this time to write your dreams and desires clearly and succinctly, and read them daily.

WAXING MOON

This is the perfect time to create a vision board. Add photos, drawings and quotes, and check in on it every day. This is a time of growth, expansion, action and progress.

FULL MOON

During the full moon, you'll be blessed with the energy of abundance and undergo a period of increased manifesting power. Use these joyful days for gratitude, celebration and forgiveness.

WANING MOON

Spend this time reducing, removing and releasing. Meditate on what you want more and less of in your life in preparation for the next moon cycle to begin.

Honour
Female Energy

*The moon phases are excellent reminders
to express gratitude for the women in your life.*

The moon is typically thought to be a feminine energy and is often associated with wisdom, fertility, mystery and power.

In some traditions she is personified as the Triple Goddess, representing the female archetypes of Maiden, Mother and Crone as she moves through her lunar phases. In traditional cultures, women would menstruate together during the dark night of the new moon.

Whether you identify as a woman or otherwise, use this time to:

- Pay respect to your feminine side

- Express gratitude to the women that birthed and nurtured you

- Gather your sisterhood and be held in love without competition or judgement

- Honour the womb and the new life it brings

- Dance wildly in nature to reconnect with mother earth

- Understand that female power is sacred and vital

I am a wild woman.
I dance with the tides of the moon.

Create a Moon Altar

It's important to have a sacred and symbolic place in your home or garden where you can focus and direct energy.

There's no right or wrong way to make a moon altar. You can set it up inside or outside, and make it elaborate or simple. All you need is a dedicated spot to call upon the moon's energy for the change and support you've been seeking.

This is where you can meditate, hold rituals and do spellwork and send your gratitude up to the moon for shining down on you night after night. Make sure it's a calm, quiet place where you will not be disturbed and where you feel truly at peace.

Create your altar in whichever way you are drawn to: try including tea lights or candles, placing a crystal to represent the moon in the centre of your altar, or sprinkling flower petals or essential oils.

Think about including the elements of earth, water, fire and air, depending on your wants and needs.

You can also add any other objects or plants that speak to you, and change them up depending on the moon's phase.

Some suggestions to get you started

CRYSTALS THAT REPRESENT THE MOON

Selenite

Opal

Moonstone

Clear quartz

Labradorite

FLOWERS THAT REPRESENT THE MOON

Jasmine

Water lilies

White roses

Moonflower

TRADITIONAL LUNAR HERBS

Fennel

Moonwort

Mugwort

Sandalwood

OTHER OBJECTS

Tarot cards

Coloured ribbon

Chalices or jars

Incense

Bells or chimes

A small bowl of salt

Know Your Moon Sign

While most people know their astrological sun sign, your moon sign can be far more revealing.

While your sun sign reflects your outward personality and your ego – how you shine your light out into the world – your moon sign, which is based on the position of the moon at your time of birth, is more hidden and subtle.

Generally regarded as the next most important influence in your horoscope chart after the sun, the moon represents your inner mood and your subconscious. This means your moon sign can reveal a lot about your personality, emotions and intuition. It's about the private self and its motivations and anxieties – essentially your internal monologue and the key to understanding your emotional profile.

To find out your moon sign, you'll need your place, date and time of birth. Since the moon changes every two and a half days, the exact time of birth is very important.

You can consult a professional astrologer or there are many free online calculators you can use.

MOON SIGN CHARACTERISTICS

- **Aries:** Impulsiveness, assertiveness
- **Taurus:** Stability, getting things done
- **Gemini:** Expressiveness, charisma
- **Cancer:** Emotions and intuition
- **Leo:** Optimism, confidence
- **Virgo:** Analytical outlook, self-care
- **Libra:** Balance, harmony
- **Scorpio:** Healing, rebirth
- **Sagittarius**: Curiosity, risk-taking
- **Capricorn:** Organisation, long-term goals
- **Aquarius:** Passion, independence
- **Pisces:** Creativity, empathy

Go Moon Bathing

Basking yourself under the moonlight can bring all kinds of physical and mental benefits.

Although little known and little practised, moon bathing is a wonderfully rejuvenating and relaxing activity that is both free and easy to do.

Stand, sit or lie outside at night so you can absorb the power of the moonlight that falls on you. If you're feeling energetic, you can absorb the moon's cosmic energy on a night walk or jog. If you can't go outdoors, position yourself near a window from where you can see the moon.

Breathe deeply and with intention: as you inhale, visualise the moon's powerful coolness, calmness and feminine protectiveness pouring down upon you. As you exhale, feel your body relax. Imagine your soul slowly becoming recharged with goodness and positive vibes and your mind becoming refreshed and renewed.

You can moon bathe during any of the lunar phases, but the best healing properties lie with the full moon and new moon cycles.

Ayurvedic wisdom holds that moon bathing is highly useful for calming 'pitta dosha', the angry and fiery temperament that causes excess heat inside the body. The cooling lunar energy is believed to be beneficial for high blood pressure, rashes and inflammatory conditions, which tend to arise as a result of excess pitta.

Practise
Moon Yoga

Get your inner glow on with gently flowing,
quieting moon salutations.

While most people know the sun salutation (surya namaskar), many won't have heard of its lesser-known lunar counterpart. Chandra namaskar (moon salutation) is a more fluid, grounding and calming sequence of yoga poses that invites you to succumb to the moon's soothing lunar energy.

There are many variations of chandra namaskar; pick one that speaks to you and works within your own range of limits and abilities. Whichever sequence you choose, it is best performed at night when the moon is visible as it'll help you wind down and get your body ready for a restful night's sleep. It's also an excellent choice for those days when you're feeling stressed, overstimulated or depleted.

Ideally, you should position yourself so you can see the moon or even do your practice outdoors. If you are indoors, ensure the lights are low – perhaps light a few candles for ambience or string up some fairy lights – and create a soothing environment with soft music and chanting.

Begin your practice with a short meditation to cultivate your connection with the divine feminine. Tune into a sense of devotion as you honour all the phases of the moon and the cycles of your life.

As you start the sequence, use the quiet and flowing movements to draw your attention.

New Moon

—

*Plant the seeds
of your future dreams*

WHAT TO EXPECT:

A cosmic reset.

THIS IS THE TIME TO:

Set intentions and launch new projects.

FOCUS ON:

*Grounding yourself and finding
a sense of direction.*

WORK ON:

Finding your own truth.

AVOID:

Making any rash or impulsive decisions.

The new moon occurs about once a month when the moon is between the earth and the sun, leaving the side of the moon that faces us in darkness. In fact, new moons are only visible during a solar eclipse.

In the day or two following the new moon, the moon slowly appears as a very thin sliver of silvery light, swelling over the next two weeks to the radiance of the full moon.

Just as the new moon represents the start of the lunar cycle, it also symbolises new beginnings. The new moon represents a second chance and a blank slate, where you can reboot, set intentions and launch new projects. This is why the new moon is the perfect time to meditate, journal, organise and plan your next move.

Many people react unconsciously to this lunar energy, intuitively starting new ventures and projects around this time. However, by actively harnessing and responding to the energy of the new moon, you can make even more impactful changes. The new moon's purifying energy will aid you in your reflection and help you correct your course in life.

This is the time for fresh starts, new businesses and setting goals. It's an opportunity to take ownership of what you want to manifest and to commit to the actions, thoughts and behaviours necessary to get you there. The three days after the new moon are the most powerful times for rituals, meditation and self-reflection, so plan accordingly.

Only in the darkness of an ending does the new moon arise.

What to Do During the New Moon

This is the ideal time for self-reflection, course correction and goal setting.

DO... DREAM BIG

Write down your goals and dreams for the upcoming month and send them out into the universe for assistance in realising them. The new moon is an excellent time to work on your career and your personal development, though any rituals around new beginnings, banishing the past and moving forwards are good to do at this time.

DO... CREATE A SACRED SPACE

Creating an altar or sanctuary in your home is an excellent way to direct your new moon energy. Clear a space and set in it any objects or pictures that remind you of what you're calling in with the new moon. Candles, aromatherapy oils and crystals can also help ground your energy. Refer to page 28 for more information.

DO... SLOW DOWN

Commit to a set of practices or habits that allow you to reflect and plant a few seeds of intention. This could include meditating, yoga or stargazing. This moment of calm could even be as simple as lighting a candle each morning or filling your diffuser with your favourite essential oil. It's about briefly pressing pause every day to recharge and reset.

DO... START SOMETHING NEW

Think about where you'd like to be in life and figure out the path to get there. Perhaps that means looking for a new job or identifying a new course. Maybe it involves joining a dating app. Start anything and everything you feel passionate about as this is the perfect time to plant the seeds for your future life.

What Not to Do During the New Moon

The energy of a new moon is your blank page for new beginnings; funnel your energy into starting, not stopping.

DON'T... LOOK BACKWARDS

Since the new moon brings change and new perspectives, it's important to focus on the future rather than dwelling on the past. Remember that you cannot change what is already done; instead use this time to redirect your path to wherever you want and need to be.

DON'T... SAY NO

This is not a time to be closing yourself off from new opportunities or friendships. Rather, make sure you say YES to any experiences the universe puts in your path. What you open yourself up to now could end up defining your life.

DON'T... QUIT SOMETHING YOU LOVE

While you may want to jump straight into your new, improved life, be mindful of what you let go of. Some things may be more important to your life than you realise, and giving up on them during a new moon may prove to be a waste of energy.

DON'T... MAKE RASH DECISIONS

Although the new moon heralds change, be careful not to be impulsive. Consider your desires carefully and focus on the things you are passionate about. This is not a time for knee-jerk reactions to what may not be going well in your life, but a time to reflect on your dreams, relationships and goals.

Don't worry if you're making waves simply by being yourself. The moon does it all the time.

Scott Stabile

Set Your New Moon Intentions

Intentions and affirmations hold power, so take care when considering what you truly want.

1.

Think of the things you want to draw into your life over the next lunar cycle. This is your opportunity to conjure what may have previously seemed out of reach, so be bold in your thoughts and actions.

2.

Use the following pages to jot down your thoughts. Let the words flow from you without restraint. Once your mind is clear, refine your notes to just three to five intentions and make them as specific as possible.

3.

Once you have your final list, write or draw these intentions on two small pieces of paper.

4.

Place a white candle in a small bowl of water with a pinch of sea salt (the wick and top of the candle should be above the water). Light it.

5.

Take one of the pieces of paper, set it on fire and place into the water once it's nearly burned out. Visualise your dreams soaring up to the heavens.

6.

Anoint the other piece of paper with your favourite essential oil, fold the paper into four and place in a safe place, such as in a box with a favourite crystal on your altar.

Release Your Intentions to the Universe

The cosmos is always listening and it wants to support you in achieving your dreams.

HOW TO PREPARE

Draw on the power of breath, breathing out to release any negative emotions and breathing in the possibilities of the future.

On the following pages write some simple affirmations that have meaning for you, using the ones opposite to guide and inspire you. It's important that you choose words that resonate with you and that match up with the intentions you have already written.

WHAT TO DO

Spend five minutes at the start and end of each day during the new moon period revisiting your intentions and then repeating your affirmations out loud in nature or near

a window. By doing this, you will encourage and motivate yourself to keep progressing on your chosen path.

When you are finished, sit quietly for a few minutes and enjoy your positive and peaceful state of mind. You'll feel ever-increasing power in your words as the moon's light builds.

BE SURE TO

Believe in what you are releasing or requesting. If you do not have faith that what you are trying to manifest is possible, then it won't be.

'I reclaim my power and embrace new beginnings'

—

'I am reborn with this new moon'

—

'I invite all forms of abundance into my life'

—

'I let go of what is no longer serving me'

—

'I have the power to shape my reality'

—

'I give myself space to grow and learn'

—

'I trust that I am on the right path'

—

'I am inspired by the world around me'

Purify Your Space in the New Moon

Purge anything that doesn't serve you;
by letting go you will make space for the new.

CLEAN YOUR FRONT DOOR

Do this with the intention of new beginnings and inviting in what you are wanting to manifest.

SMUDGE YOUR HOME

Make sure the doors and windows are open so there's an exit point for any bad vibes. Light a sage smudging stick (you can buy these or make your own) and let it burn for 20 seconds before blowing out the flame. Starting at the front door, move through each room, wafting the smoke all around especially in the corners and up to the ceiling. This symbolic act takes negative and unwanted energy out of the house.

CLEAR YOUR MIND

Meditate, paying attention to your breath as it goes in and out. Be aware of your thoughts, emotions and sensations — whatever it is that's passing through your body and mind. Afterwards, take a detox bath (see page 60) to clear your field of any negative energies.

LIGHT A CANDLE

Ask the universe to shine light into your life on this dark new moon and all the ones that follow it, then let the candle burn out on its own.

Three things cannot be long hidden: the sun, the moon and the truth.

Buddha

New Moon Detox Bath Recipe

Soak in the waters of change as you cleanse yourself both physically and energetically.

INGREDIENTS

1-2 cups Epsom or mineral salts

1 teaspoon calendula flowers

1 teaspoon lavender flowers

1 teaspoon rose petals

1 cup your choice of milk

A few drops of your favourite essential oils (try lavender for relaxation, jasmine for positivity and frankincense for purification)

METHOD

Add all ingredients to your bath water.

Try adding a moonstone to bring out your inner goddess. Choose selenite for a deeper cleansing or rose quartz for unconditional self-love. Place the crystals around the edge of the bath to form a gorgeous self-care altar.

Light a candle at the foot of the bath, and play relaxing ambient music or chants.

Meditate, focussing on any unwanted or residual energy and imagining it seeping into the water. Once you're feeling relaxed and cleansed, pull the plug and let any discomforts or frustrations drain away.

Waxing Moon

—

*Make quick decisions
and act boldly*

WHAT TO EXPECT:

Challenges, decisions and action.

THIS IS THE TIME TO:

Be flexible in your thinking.

FOCUS ON:

*The intentions you set
during the new moon.*

WORK ON:

Achieving your to-do list.

AVOID:

*Losing your cool when things
don't go to plan.*

The waxing moon, so called because its illuminated area is increasing, occurs after the new moon and lasts through to its full glory during the full moon.

After the previous period of setting intentions and launching new projects, it's time to start working to achieve them. Look out for flashes of guidance from the universe, moments of clarity, potential collaborations and serendipitous meetings. You may be able to find messages in the smallest or unlikeliest of encounters or experiences.

Although you might be fully focussed on achieving your desires, be prepared to find some obstacles in your path. While any disruptions to your plans may be frustrating, remember that the road to happiness and fulfilment is rarely smooth. In fact, by forcing you to remain focussed on your end goal, you'll ride the momentum that's underway due to the abundant growing power of the moon.

Focus on progressing any projects you're working on, and try to stay calm when issues come at you out of nowhere. Be prepared to make big decisions, pivot quickly and be flexible in your thinking. This phase of the moon will help you realise what you need to re-evaluate, give up or change direction on.

Although things may not unfold the way you imagined, keep adjusting, refining and editing and trust that the universe is working in your favour.

The water in the stream may have changed many times, but the reflection of the moon and the stars remains the same.

Rumi

What to Do During the Waxing Moon

Use this growth phase to embrace all your hopes and wishes and get your plans in motion.

DO... WRITE AN ACTION PLAN

Use your moon phase calendar to identify the days in this waxing phase (approximately two weeks), and plan one action each day until the moon is full. This could include listening to podcasts, going somewhere new, setting a morning meditation or doing candlelight spells – whatever will help you achieve the goals you've set. Write down any and all ideas so you don't forget them.

DO... GET TO WORK

This is likely the lunar period where you'll have an onslaught of new ideas, and when you're most able to effectively act on them. Find pictures that represent your goals and use them to create a vision board. Take decisive action on behalf of your intended desires, and go after what you want with your whole heart.

DO... CHARGE YOUR MAGICAL TOOLS

The waxing moon's light will be sending out joyful manifesting energy, so this is a perfect time to harness its power. Get out your crystals, journals, herbs, incantations, tarot cards and whatever else you use as guides on your spiritual journey and place them outside overnight under the moonlight. In the morning, they'll be charged and ready to go.

DO... MOVE QUICKLY

It is essential to keep making forward strides in order to harness the momentum that's underway and catch onto the abundant growing power of the moon. Pick up the pace and make sure you bring new things, people and relationships into your life.

What Not to Do During the Waxing Moon

The decisions you make now will help propel your actions in the right direction.

DON'T... RESIST CHANGE

There's no need to be set in your ways. If the universe is telling you that your direction is not right, don't be scared to change your intentions from the previous week. Identify any issues that have arisen since the new moon and adjust your goals accordingly.

DON'T... FORCE CONNECTIONS

Relax and let the universe guide you on your path. When you work with the moon's abundant energy, magic can happen in the most surprising places with very little effort. Since the universe works in mysterious ways, you may just be on a different route to the same destination.

DON'T... TURN INWARDS

This is time to tap into the moon's ancient wisdom by asking for help and guidance. You don't need to do this on your own – remember that the moon is there waiting for you. Take a moment each night during this phase to close your eyes and send a question or request up into the night's sky.

DON'T... GIVE UP

Although things might not be unfolding as you thought they would, do not throw in the towel. Take advantage of the added motivation that this moon phase brings: try to face adversity with a resolute mind, find workarounds and embrace challenges. Only by working through issues will you achieve personal growth.

Write a Gratitude List

Acknowledge what you're grateful for and you will receive more beauty, love and positivity into your life.

1.

Buy a new journal or write in the space provided here. Having a dedicated place to record your thoughts and feelings will help you do this activity regularly.

2.

Write by hand rather than typing on your computer or your phone. This will help you remain thoughtful and aware. It's well known that you invest more of your time and energy into something when you feel a connection to it.

3.

Keep it simple. It's vital that this doesn't feel like a chore, so start with just a few small things that you're grateful for. You can build on this as you get more used to thinking in this way.

4.

Keep your sentences as short or as long as you like – there are no rules around how to mark your gratitude.

5.

Reflect on what you've written and think about how these things are helping you achieve your goals. This introspection will aid you as the moon continues its cycle and gains in power.

6.

Acknowledge the power of positivity. What you're grateful for may seem to be insignificant right now, but these tiny seeds will grow and flourish.

Let the waters settle, you will see stars and moon mirrored in your being.

Rumi

Pull Oracle Cards For Divine Guidance

Take a moment during the waxing moon phase to close your eyes and send your questions into the universe.

HOW TO PREPARE

Keep your oracle cards in a sacred space, such as on your altar or special shelf in your home along with your crystals. Lay out your cards and infuse them with your energy by moving your hands over them. Now take a moment to pause and connect with yourself. Use this time to clarify exactly what you're asking for.

WHAT TO DO

Shuffle the deck, then cut it into three piles and restack them into a single pile. Next, spread the cards out and hover over them with your hand until you feel a pull or connection. Take out this card and use what is on it for inspiration or insight into a situation. Trust your intuition and try not to overthink!

WHAT TO LOOK FOR

Look for messages from the universe in the themes, pictures, words, phrases or symbols on the card. Did any distinct feelings come up as you read it? Or has it inspired actions or thoughts? The card's sentiment may resonate with you or leave you with more questions than you had to begin with. Either way, it'll likely be a good guide as to your next steps.

IDEAS OF WHAT TO ASK

What do I need to know today?
What is keeping me from moving forward?
What is my lesson in this situation?
Where should I go next?
What do I need most right now?
What will help me achieve my goals?
What is my biggest block to success?
Where should I be looking for answers?

Do Some Candle Magic

Candle magic is one of the simplest forms of spellcasting and can be a complementary ritual during the waxing moon.

While candle magic can involve simply lighting a candle and reading over your intentions, you can also dive deeper into this soul work.

Set yourself up at your altar or find a quiet, safe space to work. Choose the candle you wish to use (use the list on page 82 to help you) and focus your intention into a short word or image. Use a pin or needle to carefully engrave this into the candle wax. Alternatively, write or draw your intention on a small piece of paper and place it beneath your candle holder.

When this is done, hold your candle in your right hand while visualising the outcome you are working towards. Then place the candle into the holder, light it and ask it to guide you. It's essential that you speak aloud to your candle, even if you prefer to whisper. Speak your magic to find your truth!

Pay attention to the way the candle burns. It might burn small or tall, flicker or have multiple flames. Two flames could mean someone from the spirit world is guiding you on your journey, while a candle that burns tall and strong signals that your wish will be fulfilled. A dancing flame may indicate potential problems ahead. Even the colours found in the flame may give you a clue about the message you are being given.

If you so desire, you can read the candle wax by dripping the melted wax into a bowl of ice-cold water. The wax will harden and form shapes that you can use as guides to answer your questions.

Candle colour symbolism

WHITE
Purity and truth

RED
Love, lust

GOLD
Financial gain,
business endeavours

GREEN
Abundance and fertility

PINK
Friendship

PURPLE
Ambition

SILVER
Reflection, intuition

BLUE
Health and longevity

BLACK
Banishing negativity,
transforming grief

Be the light.

A Waxing Moon Ritual for Clarity

Fine-tune your desires in order to take your intentions from idea to reality.

Get a bowl of water and a pen.

Relax your body and mind and meditate on the bowl of water. Think about the intentions you set during the new moon, how you plan to achieve your goals with integrity and honour, and identify anything that might be holding you back.

As thoughts drift into your mind, jot them down in the journal space on the next pages. As your pen writes out the thought, visualise it leaving your mind and anchoring firmly itself on the page, then quickly move onto the next thought.

After you've written down each thought, return your focus to the bowl of water. Continue to do this exercise for 5-10 minutes or until your mind is calm and clear.

Look at the list of things you wrote down. Start with any negative emotions or thoughts and imagine submerging these in the bowl of water and washing away your fears or worries. By consciously choosing to release the old stories that get in our way, we can create clarity and a healthy new mindset.

Finally, take the positive thoughts that will help you manifest your dreams and pin them onto your vision board or place them on your sacred altar. Repeat out loud to yourself that everything is going to be okay and that you are the master of your future.

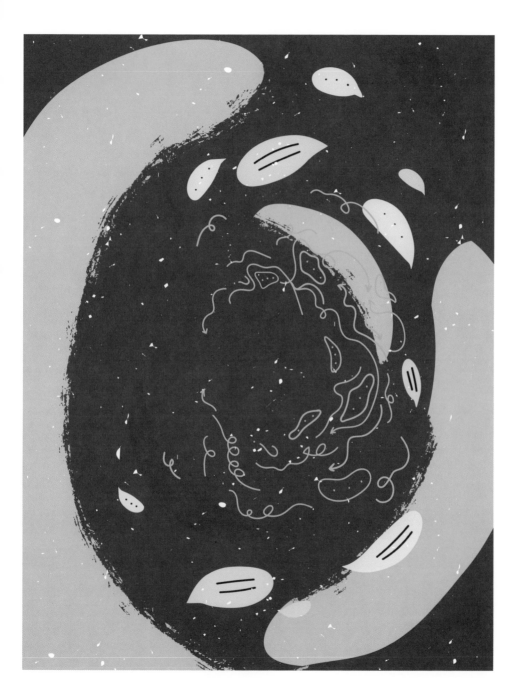

Full Moon

—

*Time to reap and harvest
your rewards*

WHAT TO EXPECT:
*Abundant energy and
transformation.*

THIS IS THE TIME TO:
*Visualise your desires coming
to fruition.*

FOCUS ON:
Staying calm and unruffled.

WORK ON:
*Evaluating, assessing,
cleansing and recharging.*

AVOID:
*Jumping straight into the
next new thing.*

The full moon occurs when the moon is opposite the sun and is as close as it can be to being fully illuminated.

As the pinnacle of the moon's cycle, the full moon is seen as an especially transformational time. The moon's energy is at its peak and is very powerful. While this energy lasts for about three days before and after the lunation, the moon is technically only full for a moment, when its face is completely illuminated.

Just as the full moon lights up our planet, it also shines a light on things you may not have noticed or acknowledged around you. This is an excellent time to evaluate what's going on and get focussed on what you want. Take some time to notice what has and hasn't come fruition in your life yet.

At this time of high spiritual and universal energies, some people may be fuelled with creativity and inspiration. This is why the full moon is a good time to act boldly; use this time to release your inhibitions and step out into the world.

However, the full moon can be a disruptive time for others, perhaps displaying as tiredness or anxiety or simply making you feel a little unsettled. Emotions definitely run high during this period, so it's important to find ways to ground yourself amid the onslaught of energetic forces.

Keep an eye on your mental state so you can take the necessary steps to make sure that you remain in a state of balance.

Happy full moon, witches!

What to Do During the Full Moon

Use this time wisely to make the most of the powerful energies that are swirling around you.

DO... STAY CALM

Many people feel a bit scattered during this moon phase because the lunar energy is so potent. This means you must find a way to bring calmness into your space in order to harness the forces to your benefit. Take some deep cleansing breaths, refresh your space with a sage wand and set some time aside for relaxation and introspection.

DO... COUNT YOUR BLESSINGS

This is a powerful time of appreciation, where you should acknowledge the beauty of the world and everything around you. You may feel a desire to express your creativity, bliss out in sensual activities or take a luxurious bath to unwind. Sit with your thoughts, celebrate your successes and send your gratitude into the universe.

DO... CREATE A CRYSTAL GRID

Arrange your cleansed crystals in a sacred geometric configuration (create your own design or look for templates online) and create an affirmation as the focus of your grid. If you like, include leaves or flowers or other natural objects. Activate the energy of the grid by using a clear quartz crystal point to link the energy of the crystals.

DO... HOLD A MOON CIRCLE

The full moon is a time of synergy, and sharing the experience with others makes us realise that the possibilities in life are endless. Attend or organise a full moon circle ceremony as a powerful way to bring healing to yourself and to the group. Use this time to set intentions, actively listen and collectively decide what to release.

What Not to Do During the Full Moon

Don't be afraid to push back in order to reach the pinnacle of your spiritual and energetic endeavours.

DON'T... FEEL OVERWHELMED

When the sun and moon oppose each other during a full moon, this can result in uncomfortable tension and friction. During this time emotions and dreams are often amplified, but there's no need to feel overburdened. Instead, embrace this time as having the potential for greater vision and possibility.

DON'T... LISTEN TO NAYSAYERS

One of the most beautiful aspects of the full moon is that this is when your intuition is at its peak. Trust in yourself and don't be swayed by the opinions of others who may not have your best interests at heart. Stay open to new elements and experiences entering your life and surround yourself with positivity.

DON'T... HOLD ONTO EMOTIONAL BAGGAGE

This is the perfect time to let go of anything that is not in alignment with your values and plans. Identify behaviours, people and patterns that aren't getting you any closer to the life you want. If something or someone doesn't sit right with your heart, just let them go.

DON'T... START SOMETHING NEW

As the full moon represents fruitfulness and completeness, use this time to tie up loose ends and wrap any projects up. Finish off odd jobs, tick off the final things on your to-do list and make space for what is to come. Look back on what you have achieved and acknowledge your efforts.

Let the beauty of the full moon inspire the change you desire.

Full Moon Reflection

Shine some light on what may not be serving you, and clear space for what you want to attract.

YOU ARE WORTHY

Think about how important you are to those around you and how you express your energy to the world. Know you deserve love and acceptance in life and that you must live your life as authentically and as bravely as possible.

YOUR TRIBE IS EVERYTHING

Write down the ways in which you are not only receiving support from others but are supporting them too. Recognise the people who are helping you along your journey, and be sure to tell them what they mean to you.

YOU ARE THANKFUL

Express gratitude for how the seeds you planted during the new moon are starting to flourish and how the path you are on in life is the perfect one for you. Know that your heart is in the right place and that your intentions are for the highest good of all involved.

YOU ARE PART OF SOMETHING BIGGER

Take time to feel connected to the beautiful natural world around you. Gaze up at the trees, breathe in the fresh air and know that there is a greater purpose to life. Use the following pages to record your thoughts.

Make Full Moon Water

Harness the full moon's potent energy to cleanse and empower yourself for the month ahead.

Take a container, such as a jam jar or favourite vase, fill it with filtered water or fresh rainwater and place it outside overnight in the direct line of the moonlight. If you wish, lay some crystals near the container for extra amplification; selenite is an excellent option for purification, while moonstone adds a calming energy.

Check which zodiac sign the moon is in, because this will affect the energy of the water.

As you set the container down on the ground, spend a few minutes meditating pure and positive thoughts. In the morning collect the container and use the charged moon water for the following.

Drink it: Take a sip or two every day, nourishing yourself with the power of the moon.

Energise your crystals with it: Soak your favourite crystals in moon water; their power will be amplified as they absorb the moon's powerful energy.

Beautify yourself with it: Place the moon water in a spray bottle, add a few drops of your favourite essential oil and use it as a face mist or perfume.

Clean your home with it: Add a few drops to your natural cleaning solutions along with a few drops of lemon or peppermint essential oil to give your home a deep energetic clearing.

Embrace the Power of Movement

The full moon is time to let go of stagnant energies and start afresh in mind, body and spirit.

DANCE LIKE NO ONE IS WATCHING

Release the built-up energy brought by the full moon by dancing it out! Leap, twirl and gyrate under the illuminated sky, drawing on the energies of ancient civilisations that worshipped its feminine energy.

SWIM IN THE MOONLIGHT

Head to the ocean, a lake, river, stream, pond or another body of water and submerge yourself. Float in the cool water and feel the healing lunar energy shine through you. Realise that by living in harmony with the lunar cycle you will learn to stop swimming against the tide.

EMBARK ON A NATURE WALK

Feel connected to the natural world by walking barefoot through nature, allowing your toes and feet to sink into the earth and breathing in the fresh air. Howl into the night and feel yourself connected to the power of the universe.

GROUND YOURSELF WITH YOGA

A full moon can often bring restless days and sleepless nights. Try some relaxing yoga poses (see page 34) that will help you slow down, find balance and align your energies.

CALL ON YOUR SPIRIT ANIMAL

Put on some soft music and summon the power of your spirit animal into your body. By moving like the animal moves, you will strengthen your connection with your sacred protector.

The full moon – the mandala of the sky.

Tom Robbins

Full Moon Tea Recipe

Use a restorative blend of herbs, spices and flowers for grounding and intuition during this lunar period.

INGREDIENTS

1 cup white peony tea leaves
½ cup dried chamomile flowers
¼ cup dried hibiscus petals
½ teaspoon dried ginger root
Sprinkle of black pepper, to taste

METHOD

Combine all ingredients in a glass jar. Stir so the ingredients are evenly distributed. Keep in a cool, dry place.

To brew, scoop one tablespoon of loose tea into an infuser or strainer. Add hot water (for added benefits use moon water) and brew for 4-5 minutes.

Enjoy a cup while reflecting on all the ways you have experienced fullness and joy in your life.

HERBS AND FLOWERS FOR THE FULL MOON

Rose	*Anise*
Nettle	*Ginger*
Chamomile	*Vanilla*
Mint	*Borage*
Hibiscus	*Basil*
Marshmallow root	*Sage*
Jasmine	*Lemon myrtle*

Come, let us have some tea and continue to talk about happy things.

Chaim Potok

Waning Moon

—

*Listen intently for direction
and guidance*

WHAT TO EXPECT:

Reflection, completion and surrender.

THIS IS THE TIME TO:

Carve out time for some self-care and rest.

FOCUS ON:

*Facing up to any shadows that
have held you back.*

WORK ON:

Letting go of what's no longer serving you.

AVOID:

Expending energy unnecessarily.

The waning moon is often represented by the crone, a powerful and wise figure who embodies acceptance and culmination. This approximately two-week-long phase is all about slowing down and connecting with yourself on the deepest level. Just as there is a time to plan, act and celebrate, now is the time to rest, release and make space.

As the light disseminates after the full moon, you will feel moved to go within and do the internal work of seeking answers and guidance. Grant yourself full permission to become increasingly committed to yourself and your needs during this time. Rest, heal and meditate, immerse yourself in spellwork and be gentle with yourself.

Allow what you no longer want to hold onto to fade away with the waning moon. Release what is not needed, reflect on what is blocking you from receiving your desired outcomes and learn to release those patterns and people. Use this opportunity to think back on the lunar cycle that has come to pass. What did you achieve? What did you fail at? What resonated the most? What have you learned?

Reread your new moon intentions (page 48) and note how you've changed and grown since you wrote them. Look back at your gratitude list (page 72) and see if there's anything you'd like to add. Then consider how you want to prepare for the next new moon.

Although the abundant energy in the earlier stages of the lunar cycle can feel the most exciting, the efforts you make now during the waning moon can bring about true and lasting change in your life.

The moon is the reflection of your heart and moonlight is the twinkle of your love.

Debasish Mridha

What to Do During the Waning Moon

Harness the cleansing power of this lunar phase to clear obstacles and release negative influences.

DO... CATCH UP ON SLEEP

This is the perfect time to rest and recuperate before the new moon, which brings fresh starts and renewed action. Although it may be difficult to sit back and believe that all will be well, be patient and trust that this is the right thing to do. It means that you'll be all the more ready when the new moon arrives.

DO... HAVE FAITH IN YOURSELF

There is only so much you can do to control an outcome, so now it is time to believe in the power of your intention and manifestation. You are a wise powerful being who has accomplished a great deal. It's time to acknowledge your growth and believe in your future.

DO... START DREAMING

If you don't already know what to focus on next, try engaging in ritual, tarot divination or meditation to determine what you require for this next moon cycle. Watch carefully for any out-of-the-ordinary signs and be sure to take on board any guidance or advice you receive.

DO... HELP OTHERS

Use the waning moon phase as a time to send blessings out into the universe. Make a donation to charity, offer to help someone in need or simply listen to someone without judgement. Although you must do these things altruistically, they will likely return to you in abundance one day.

What Not to Do During the Waning Moon

The waning moon reminds us that it's necessary to slow down, take stock and make space for the new cycle.

DON'T... IGNORE SIGNS

Reflect back on this past moon cycle and look for any messages you might've received. Perhaps a certain person kept showing up in your dreams or the same place keeps calling you back. Maybe something is stuck in your head or your inner voice keeps whispering to you. If nothing strikes you as different, perhaps it's time to ask the universe to send you a clear sign.

DON'T... MOVE TOO SOON

Although it might seem that your intentions have manifested and that your work is done, it's not quite time to jump into something new. Rest and reflect back on this past cycle and consider what you'd change or do differently.

DON'T... LIVE IN CLUTTER

This is a great time to get rid of things, both emotional and physical. Go through your wardrobe and take anything you don't wear to the Salvos. Organise, make appointments, clean your house, pay bills. Re-evaluate the relationships in your lives and set boundaries with any people who are draining you of energy.

DON'T... STRESS OUT

Relax and surrender to the universe. Some things will always be out of your control and ultimately fate must take its course. If you have to undertake a major upheaval, such as a new job or moving house, try to hold off until the very end of this lunar period.

There are better things ahead than any we leave behind.

C. S. Lewis

Waning Moon Mantra

*Each day as the moon wanes make some time
to sit with yourself in quiet contemplation.*

As you look back on the challenges and obstacles you faced during this lunar cycle, identify what held you back and address these things with an open heart and mind. Don't shy away from any negative emotions, behaviours or thoughts, but rather invite them in and use them as an opportunity to continue learning and growing.

Express gratitude to the universe that you can now see how past beliefs and habits have influenced your life. Understand that these experiences have made you who you are and that only you know the true you.

Reflection can be uncomfortable, but it can also be liberating as you develop a better understanding of yourself and your situation. Once you understand and accept, you can then move onto greater things.

Using the mantras on the opposite page as a guide, write your own mantras on the following page, using 'I am' statements that show gratitude and acceptance for the experiences you have had over this lunar cycle and the course of your life.

Repeat these phrases every day until they are deeply anchored in your heart and mind.

I AM LEARNING FROM MY
PAST EXPERIENCES

—

I AM TRANSFORMING INTO
A NEW WAY OF BEING

—

I AM FORGIVING THOSE
PEOPLE WHO HELD
ME BACK

—

I AM AT ONE WITH THE
ENERGY OF THE COSMOS

—

I AM SEEING CLEARLY AND
KNOW THE NEXT STEPS I NEED
TO TAKE

—

I AM ON MY TRUE PATH TO
FULFILMENT

I AM UNDERSTANDING THAT MY
PATH IS SOLELY MY OWN

—

I AM LETTING GO OF GRIEF,
DOUBT AND FEAR

—

I REST PEACEFULLY, KNOWING
MY TRANSFORMATION IS
NEARLY COMPLETE

—

I AM SECURE IN THE
KNOWLEDGE THAT I CAN MAKE
THE RIGHT CHOICES

—

I AM LISTENING TO MY
INNER VOICE

—

I AM HUMBLED BY THE BEAUTY
OF THE UNIVERSE

Bake Moon Cookies

These crescent-shaped biscuits will inspire you with their creativity, charm and deliciousness.

INGREDIENTS

250g plain flour
1 pinch salt
230g cold unsalted butter, cut into cubes
90g icing sugar
100g almond flour
1 tsp vanilla bean paste
A sprinkling of any herbs or spices that match your intentions (see list opposite)
Decorations (see method)

METHOD

Preheat oven to 180°C and line a baking tray with baking paper. Use a stand mixer with the paddle attachment to combine flour, salt, butter, sugar, almond flour and vanilla. Sprinkle in your chosen herbs and spices .

Mix at medium speed until a crumbly dough forms, about 1 to 2 minutes. If the dough is too crumbly add 1 to 2 tablespoons of water.

Use your hands to press the dough together and wrap it in plastic wrap. Chill for an hour in the fridge.

Roll the chilled dough into a log approximately 3cm thick. Cut the log into 4cm pieces, form the pieces into small cylinders and taper the ends. Bend each one into a crescent shape.

Place the biscuits on the baking tray. Bake for 12 to 15 minutes until the edges are golden.

Once cooled, sprinkle some moon dust (or icing sugar) on top. Alternatively, dip them in melted chocolate or decorate them with white icing and silver sprinkles for an added bonus.

Store in an airtight container until ready to serve or eat.

HERB AND SPICE SYMBOLISM

 CARDAMOM
Symbolises lust, love and fidelity

 LEMON
For cleansing, spiritual opening and removal of blockages

 THYME
Attracts loyalty, affection and the good opinion of others

 CARAWAY
Prevents your lover from straying

 NUTMEG
Attracts money, breaks hexes

 LAVENDER
Symbolises love and attraction, healing and peace

 PISTACHIO
Used for breaking love spells

 ORANGE
Signifies happiness in love and marriage

 GINGER
Brings sensuality, sexuality, personal confidence

 STAR ANISE
Increases psychic awareness and abilities

 POPPY SEED
Brings pleasure, heightened awareness, luck, invisibility

 ALMOND
Attracts wisdom, fruitfulness and prosperity

Four Steps to Break Free of Negative Patterns

The waning moon is an excellent time to shift energies and change direction.

1.

Recognise your patterns. Consider phrases you often repeat or situations you seem to regularly find yourself in. Admit to yourself that these are well-worn paths and make a conscious move in a different direction.

2.

Do a banishing spell (see page 138). This will help move any negative situations out of your life, whether that's financial issues, bad habits, toxic people or difficult work situations.

3.

Go on a detox or a cleanse. Do you need to stop drinking or start sleeping more? Do you feel you need to reset your eating habits? Do you want a general refresh? This is the time to do it as the waning moon is about getting things in order.

4.

Surround yourself with crystals. Clear quartz, rose quartz, obsidian, tourmaline, turquoise and amethyst will help you with their healing properties and allow you to maintain positive energy during this time.

Old energy is clearing. New energy is entering. Great things are coming.

Make Banishing Oil

These protective, cleansing and boosting ingredients can be used to get rid of things that no longer serve you.

The banishing oil needs to steep for some time in order to gain power and strength. Once it's ready, you can use it in many ways, from spells to protection to crystal work.

SOME SUGGESTED INGREDIENTS FOR BANISHING OIL

Garlic cloves	Ginger powder
Dried red chillies	Sage leaves
Cloves	Onion powder
Peppercorns	Rosemary oil
Lemon rind	Peppermint oil
Cinnamon powder	

Add any/all of these ingredients (choose the ones that speak to you, or are easiest to source) in the following amounts to a small jar or bottle: 1 garlic clove, 2 dried chillies, a sprinkle of spices and 5-10 drops of any oils.

Pour olive oil over to cover the ingredients, seal tightly and let the mixture steep for about two weeks. Strain and store the oil in a cool, dark place until required.

Use this oil for your banishing spells only (see page 138); it's not for consumption. It will help remove negative energies from your life and keep them from coming back. It can also work as a charm to protect you from any hexes that may have been placed against you.

Waning Moon Banishing Spell

Since the waning moon is all about release, this is an excellent time to dispel any negative energy through a banishing spell.

Dress a black spell candle with banishing oil (remember to wear gloves if your oil contains chillies!). Black candles are potent in all forms of banishing magic, for letting go of people or relationships, for transforming grief or for releasing negative emotions. If you like, you can stick thorns from any plant or tree in the sides of the candle.

Write the name of the situation or habit you wish to break free from on a piece of paper, anoint it with a few drops of banishing oil and burn it in the flame of the candle.

Say goodbye with good intent in your heart as you snuff out the flame. Sprinkle the ash from the burned paper at a crossroads to symbolise your moving on from this situation.

OTHER USES FOR BANISHING OIL

- Anoint your crystals
- Dress your spell candles
- Sprinkle outside your front door for protection
- Add to herbal blends for use in spellwork
- Place in a charm pouch or on your altar

HERRON

First Published in 2021 by Herron Book Distributors Pty Ltd
14 Manton St
Morningside
QLD 4170
www.herronbooks.com

Custom book production by Captain Honey Pty Ltd
12 Station Street
Bangalow
NSW 2479
www.captainhoney.com.au

Cataloguing-in-Publication. A catalogue record for this book is
available from the National Library of Australia

ISBN: 978-1-922432-34-6

Printed and bound in China

5 4 3 2 1   21 22 23 24 25